Famous Cat Lovers
through the centuries

Christina Hamilton

blackbird

Copyright © Christina Hamilton 2020
Published by Blackbird Digital Books
www.blackbird-books.com

A CIP catalogue record for this book is available from the British Library
ISBN 978-1-8382786-0-1

For Rosie

This book is dedicated to my own special cat, Rosie, who went to sleep for the last time on 25th April 2012. We were companions for 19 years and so I share a great love of cats with all the readers of this book.

Table of Contents

Introduction

The story of the domesticated cat covers many centuries and ranges from adoration to hatred and back full circle to mostly love.

Recent speculation seems to confirm that domestic cats are descended from one species; a Middle Eastern wildcat that lived 12,000 years ago. As the fertile crescent of the Middle East flourished, farmers began to store their grain and the mouse population expanded rapidly. The wildcats came out of the woods to hunt and so the familiar tale of the cat and mouse began. The cat was welcomed as the perfect solution to pest control, and thus began its domestication and the enduring relationship between humans and cats.

Whilst I am sure the farmers were happy that the mice were under control, all cat lovers know that cats bring far more than just an instinct for hunting small rodents.

In the US in 2017/18 nearly 32 million households owned a cat and in the UK in 2019 the PDSA estimated

10.9 million households owned a cat. This book aims to bring you surprising, interesting, and astonishing stories of that relationship. Whether they are the humble moggy or the highest pedigree, cats have always inspired and endeared themselves to people. It's not surprising that some of our most distinguished historical public figures in literature, art and politics fell in love with cats. This book ranges across the centuries and brings you the personal, private cat stories behind the public faces. I hope it will surprise and delight you as I reveal what happened behind closed doors between these famous owners and their cats.

Chapter 1 – BC/CE and 1st Century

The cult of the cat began thousands of years ago. It has been established that Egyptian culture from as early as 450BC worshipped the cat. The penalty for killing one was death and when a cat died the household would shave their eyebrows as a sign of mourning.

These were some of the observations of Herodotus, the Greek historian who lived in the 5th century BC.

He wrote *The Histories,* the first narrative record of the Ancient World. It is in his second book that he writes about Egypt and although scholars of this period have doubted his methods and authenticity he has come to be known as 'The Father of History'.

It wasn't only the cat which was worshipped by the Egyptians. Their religion was animistic; the belief that natural places, objects and animals were spiritual. Bast, or Bastet was a cat goddess and one of the most popular.

The temple at Bubastis was dedicated to her and dead cats were brought to the temple to be mummified as an offering to her.

When Cleopatra arrived in Egypt from Macedonia, she adopted not only the language but its culture. It would therefore be entirely possible that she owned a cat. Some sources name her cat as Charmain, whilst others say it was called Tivali. It was not common to name a cat. They were usually called 'mui' or 'muit' perhaps relating to the noise they make.

EMPEROR ICHIJO, *Emperor of Japan*
980AD-1011
The invention of cat cafes in Japan has given rise to many more around the world. The Japanese love cats, some even worship them, but lack of living space and long working hours prohibit many from owning them. This yearning for cat love has been satisfied with the cat

café where you pay to spend time with the cat of your choice.

There were no such restrictions for Emperor Ichijo, the 66th Emperor of Japan, who ruled from 986-1011. The high status of cats in Japan is credited to this Emperor because when he was 13 years old, in 999AD, a litter of five white kittens were born. The Emperor's favourite kitten, Myobu No Omotu was given a rank at court; Lady of the Fourth Court. A banquet was held in honour of the cat's birth and special rice cakes were made. The Emperor was so enchanted by his favourite that he decreed she was to be treated like a Royal Princess. She even had her own lady in waiting.

MOHAMMAD, *Prophet of Islam*
570 CE – 8 June 632 CE

In Islamic culture the cat has a special place in the hearts of its followers. This is due largely to the Prophet Mohammad and his favourite cat, Muezza. A particularly famous story relates how Mohammad rose from his bed as he heard the call to prayer and saw that Muezza was lying on the sleeve of his robe. He cut off the sleeve rather than disturb the cat. Such was Mohammad's devotion to Muezza that he allowed her to rest in his lap during his sermons. He also drank from the cat's water and washed himself with it. Legend also says that the 'm' marking on the forehead of a tabby cat was made by the Prophet resting his hand on its forehead.

The teachings of Islam state that Muslims must not trade or sell cats for money; they can drink the same water as cats as their saliva is harmless, unless impurities are visible in its mouth. They are free to live with cats so long as they feed and water them and treat them well and allow them to roam freely.

Chapter 2 – 1ˢᵗ to 5ᵗʰ Century

The adoration and love shown towards cats by Egypt and Asia was, to some extent, adopted by the Romans. Their conquest of Egypt meant they would have seen how much the cat was venerated. The exportation of cats was forbidden by the Egyptians and if caught, the penalty was death. The ships at the ports were searched before being allowed to leave to make sure there were no cats. It is believed that the Phoenicians, who were the largest traders in the area, managed to smuggle them out and transport the cats to Greece, Rome and Northern Europe. The cat's skill in killing rodents would have been highly appreciated by the crew of ships transporting grain. In Rome, before the importation of cats, they used weasels to kill rodents and cats were kept as pets and not hunters. Their skill and reputation for killing vermin meant that by the 5th century they had taken over in the home as both pets and hunters.

It was the Romans who brought cats to Britain when they began invading in 43 CE and became total rulers in 87CE. The Roman legions relied on cats to protect their food supplies and travelled with them as hunters and companions. In the late 1960s, excavation of an Ancient Roman Fort in Scotland, Fort Bothwellhaugh, recovered brick fragments with the imprint of a cat's paws.

After the fall of the Roman Empire in circa 476CE it was the spread of Christianity throughout Europe and Britain that saw a downturn in both the cat's reputation and popularity. The gradual adoption of Christianity in the years 500-1000CE meant the pagan belief that all animals had spirits was consistently denied and discredited by Christians. Belief in animal spirits was declared evil by the Christian church. As Christianity grew over the next centuries the attack on cats and often their owners as being sent from the devil spread across Europe

Chapter 3 – 5th to 15th Century

The Middle Ages, from the 5th to 15th Century were the worst of times for cats and their reputations in Europe. Henry I of England in the 11th century recognised their value as pest control and declared it illegal to kill a cat. If you were caught you were fined 60 bushels of corn. During the Middle ages, the dominance of Christianity throughout Medieval Europe and beyond grew. Any other religion was not tolerated, was challenged and destroyed. Throughout the whole of this period there were Crusades and witch hunts when many people were slaughtered alongside their cats. Many of those killed were denounced as witches and heretics, many of whom were women with their cats.

Control of household vermin by cats meant that women became associated as their owners. The Church at this time encouraged the condemnation of women as sinful, as Eve was in Adam's fall from Grace in the Garden of Eden. The Papal bull Vox in Roma published in 1233 by Pope Gregory IX denounced cats – especially black cats – as evil and in league with Satan.

When the Plague came to Europe in the 14[h] Century, there were few surviving cats. This meant that the black rats whose fleas carried the disease were able to roam freely. It might be that with vermin control the outcome may have been different but instead 30-60% of Europe's population died. During this time there were many witch-hunts in Europe and England and any alternative religious ideas stamped out, including the slaughter of the Cathars in Southern France and the Knights Templar.

The last 'witch' hangings in England of two women were as late as 1682, the year that the King of France stopped any further witch trials. The English Witchcraft Act was only repealed in 1736.

Chapter 4 – 16th and 17th Century

It appears that the appetite for witch-hunts was becoming less during this period. Certainly, the following historical figures didn't have any problems with being cat owners.

NOSTRADAMUS, *Mystic*
1503-1566

In December 1503 the French mystic Nostradamus was born and named Michel de Nostredame. Originally a doctor, he became famous because of his healing powers during the Bubonic plague when his herbal remedy helped towns to recover. In 1550, the year of

Shakespeare's birth, he began to produce an annual Almanac which contained predictions of the future, based on astrology and his meditations. They also contained quatrains (four-line verses) and were extremely popular and consolidated his earlier fame. His well-known prophecies not only stem from his Almanacs but from a series of 10 books called *Centuries* which he claimed would forecast the next two thousand years of humanity. The first seven were published in 1555, but the last three would not be published until his death in 1566. I am sure that Nostradamus himself could never have predicted that these books and almanacs would continue to intrigue and remain popular down the centuries.

Today, in the 21st century, there are many websites dedicated to explaining and analysing his writings. Whilst Nostradamus' visions during meditation are said to have informed his writings, there are some that say it was a small grey cat that had the most influence. Maybe it was fate or the stars aligning that brought her to his door. Despite his initial rejection, he found she was still there on his return. Unable to open his door without picking her up, she began to purr. Once inside the house, beside the fireplace, she began to work her charms and he decided she could stay. He named her Marie, after his favourite aunt. Every evening Nostradamus would work and some believe he began talking to her about his ideas. If she didn't like something, she would bite his quill but gave her approval by purring and rubbing his hand. Of course, it is not possible to seriously reference this particular anecdote or even to determine if he had a cat called Marie. He is also credited with having a cat called Grimalkin, but they may be one and the same. The origin of the name relates to the colour grey or *gris* in French and *malkin*, an ancient word for a cat. The name appears in William Baldwin's novel *Beware The Cat* published in 1570, the first English novel. It features cats as the main characters. We will never know the truth about this charming story. It's hard not to speculate that current conspiracy and end of the world theories based on the predictions of Nostradamus might just have been based on the playful whim of one of our furry friends.

CARDINAL RICHELIEU *French First Minister to Louis XIII* 1585-1642

Cardinal Richelieu, born Armand Jean du Plessis in 1585, grew up to become the First Minister to King Louis XIII. This powerful and politically astute player in the convoluted world of 17th Century European politics appeared to be austere and uncompromising. In Alexander Dumas' 19th century novel *The Three Musketeers* the Cardinal is depicted as the chief protagonist and villain and this portrayal became his legacy. During this violent period in French history the witch hunts and trials were used by many, including the Cardinal, to eliminate their enemies. It seems ironic, given the association between witches and cats, that the Cardinal was in fact a passionate cat lover.

It is believed that he built a cattery for his cats at Versailles, that they lived in a room next to his bedroom and had two servants to look after them.

The fourteen cats were all living at the time of his death in 1642 and we know their names and something of their characters. Soumise was the favourite; Mounard le Fougueux, angry and unpredictable; Ludovic le Cruel, named for his capture and torture of rats; Mimi-Paillon was a fluffy angora and tiger-like. Ludoviska came from Poland and Rubis sur L'Ongle, was a very tidy cat and loved her milk so much she drank every drop; Serpolet was a sun worshipper. Pyrame and Thisbe were named after the ill-fated lovers as they loved to curl up together to sleep.

The story of the naming of Racan and Perruque is hilarious. Monsieur Racan, an academic, put on his wig before his appointment with Richelieu. During his meeting he began to suffer pains in his scalp and on lifting his wig found two kittens. Richelieu immediately adopted them and called one after the academic and the other Perruque which is French for wig.

There are many paintings and drawings depicting Richelieu with his cats, so that part of his history we must assume to be true, although most of these were painted after his death. Whilst some people believe that he left two servants a large sum of money to look after his cats after his death, there is no proof of this. A list of bequests from a will he made in May 1642 does not mention cats, although there is a line at the bottom which leaves 292,000 livres as bequests to servants and other individuals. This bequest was maybe added later as he did not die until December of 1642. Whilst the Cardinal's cats were much loved during his life, after his death it seems there was no affection for them as far as the Swiss Guard were concerned. It is understood that they murdered all 14 cats, either as revenge against all the witches executed by the Cardinal or because, as has been suggested, they got tired of feeding them. A sad end to what is a charming story which shows that Richelieu was maybe not quite so bad as his reputation suggests.

SIR ISAAC NEWTON, *Physicist*
1643-1727

Sir Isaac Newton was born in a time of turmoil during the English Civil War. During his early life, the world turned upside down with the execution of Charles I and then the restoration of the monarchy by his son, Charles II in 1660. It could be said that Newton himself was a revolutionary as the publication of his book Mathematical Principles of Natural Philosophy in 1647 at the age of 44 began to revolutionise thinking about the principles of physical laws. There are some who called Newton a genius, mostly fellow scientists, but the public know him best as the inventor of the law of gravity by observing an apple falling from a tree. This was verified by his acquaintance William Stukely, who wrote in 1752 that Newton had told him the story, although not that the apple had hit him on the head.

The other invention claimed to be by Newton, the cat flap, is not so easily verified, although it appears to have become entrenched in popular culture. The only written source available is a magazine published in Boston in 1863 called *The Monthly Religious Magazine* Vol. 29-30 under Random Readings. The reader is informed that an anecdote relayed by *The Country Parson* (a handbook on pastoral care) illustrates that Newton became tired of opening and closing his study door for his pet cat and kitten and so proceeded to cut a large and a small hole in the study door. It appears that common sense and clear thinking evaded the great man at this point as the cat proceeded to pass through the hole followed by her kitten through the same hole.

Later versions of this story place the scene in Newton's laboratory in Cambridge and it is embellished by the addition of a piece of felt over the holes so that the cats cannot let light into the room as they enter and exit.

Confusing matters more, in a letter written in 1727 by his assistant Dr. Humphrey Newton, he observes that Sir Isaac Newton 'kept neither Dog nor Cat in his Chamber'. As Humphrey worked with him for only five years from 1685, it's possible that Newton could easily have acquired a cat later. To further add to the mystery, there are claims by contemporaries of Newton's that some years after his death there were two cat-sized holes in the laboratory door. The name of his cat, Spitface or Spithead is not easy to verify either, but it is an unusual name. Any cat who is smart enough to outwit Sir Isaac Newton deserves a memorable name. The original story, written in 1863 of Isaac Newton and the invention of the cat flap in *The Monthly Religious Magazine* can be accessed at bit.ly/2THVoAt **P.298**

Chapter 5 – 18th Century

DR. SAMUEL JOHNSON, *Author*
1709-1784

Dr. Samuel Johnson was an author, poet, literary critic and lexicographer. His famous *Dictionary of the English Language* took him nine years to write. Although not the first English dictionary, it became the most used for the next 150 years. Whilst the dictionary brought him success and popularity, it is *The Life of Samuel Johnson*, written by his friend James Boswell, which gives the reader an insight into his personal life and especially the love he had for his cat Hodge. Although, as Boswell tells us, Johnson had other cats that he liked better, he believed that Hodge was 'a very fine cat'. Hodge was indulged by Johnson in his love for oysters, so much so that he would go and purchase them himself. In the 18th century oysters were cheap and plentiful and the food of the poor.

Lily was Johnson's second favourite cat. In a letter written by Johnson in 1738, he describes a white kitten called Lily, saying she is 'well behaved'. It is not known definitively in which period of Johnson's life Hodge featured, but we do know, as witnessed by Boswell that when Hodge was dying Johnson went out and bought some valerian (a form of cat nip) to ease his suffering. If not his favourite cat, then Hodge has certainly become one of the most famous of Johnson's cats. In 1788 Percival Stockdale published *An Elegy on The Death of Dr Johnson's Favourite Cat* and from this we learn something of Hodge's love for Johnson:

Who, by his master when caressed
Warmly his gratitude expressed;
And never failed his thanks to purr
Whene'er he stroked his sable fur.

In more recent years Hodge has been further immortalised in bronze as he sits on top of a plinth outside Samuel Johnson's house in Gough Square in London. This statue was unveiled in 1997. Hodge sits beside an oyster and on top of a copy of Johnson's *Dictionary of the English Language* and the inscription

reads 'a very fine cat indeed'. The house at 17 Gough Square, EC4 is open to the public and has its own website
http://www.drjohnsonshouse.org/index.html

HORACE WALPOLE, *MP, Art Historian, Author* 1717-1797

Horace Walpole, born Horatio, was the youngest son of the first British Prime Minister, Sir Robert Walpole. He became an MP, art historian and author. On the death of his nephew he became the 4th Earl of Orford. The obligatory Grand Tour, essential for any young aristocrat in the 18th century, was undertaken from 1739-41. Ahead of his time, and no doubt influenced by his travels, he built Strawberry Hill, a Gothic revival mansion in Twickenham in 1749. It took several years to complete and is one of his continuing legacies. It is open to the public throughout the year.
Find out when at
http://www.strawberryhillhouse.org.uk/visit-us/

His gothic credentials were further cemented in 1794 when he published *The Castle of Otranto,* a gothic romance. It is not known where his love of cats and dogs came from. He was so upset at the death of his tabby cat Selima it prompted his friend Thomas Gray, a celebrated poet, to write a mock elegy. It is called *Ode on the Death of a Favourite Cat, Drowned in a Tub of*

Gold Fishes. It tells the story of how Selima's curiosity killed her by trying to catch the goldfish in a large Chinese ceramic bowl. In the last verse Gray issues a warning to other cats about the dangers of being too bold.

This charming poem can be viewed at https://bit.ly/38qsv0Z.

It is not known whether this elegy was any comfort to Walpole but Thomas Gray certainly immortalised Selima. William Blake was commissioned to illustrate Gray's poems including Selima's Ode. Reproductions of the watercolours are contained in a book published by Christopher Frayling in 2009 called *Horace Walpole's Cat*. They can also be accessed here https://bit.ly/3j5O5Qh

An illustration of the bowl can be accessed at https://bit.ly/3jdv9O1. On a pedestal below the bowl is the first stanza of Thomas Gray's ode;

'Twas on this lofty vase's side,
Where China's gayest art has dy'd
The azure flow'rs that blow,
Demurest of the tabby kind,
The pensive Selima reclin'd,
Gaz'd on the lake below.'

It may well be that the enduring mythology of cats' fascination with goldfish began with Selima and Thomas Gray's touching elegy.

MARIE ANTOINETTE, *Queen of France & Navarre*
1755-1793
On May 8 1895, a Maine Coon cat (also known as an American Long hair) called Cosey won the first ever cat show in the USA. So, what has Cosey to do with Marie Antoinette, you may ask? Well, King Louis XVI of France and his wife Marie Antoinette owned six cats. Their names are lost to time but a telling detail about their domestic set-up shows how loved they were. The cats were allowed to roam the tables during court gatherings, nibbling on the choicest morsels. They were

indulged, like many domestic pets, emphasising their high position in the household hierarchy.

These were no ordinary moggies though. They were Turkish Angoras and they are believed to have been involved in the origin of one of the oldest North American natural breeds, the Maine Coon.

According to his family records, Captain Stephen Clough sailed into Paris on his lumber trade ship *Sally* during the height of the French Revolution. Like a lot of Americans, he was sympathetic to the French nobility's persecution at the hands of Robespierre during the Reign of Terror. He became involved in a plan to rescue Marie Antoinette and smuggle her aboard the *Sally* bound for Wiscasset, Maine. Ahead of the voyage her silver, china, and other valuable possessions, including her cats, were loaded onto the ship. As we all know, the plan failed and she was guillotined at the Place de la Revolution on 16th October 1793. Captain Clough sailed with the Queen's cargo and successfully landed at Wiscasset, Maine. It is believed that the cats were then released to roam freely. They mated with short-hair breeds and this led to the creation of the Maine Coon, now recognised as the official State Cat of Maine.

SIR WALTER SCOTT, *Author*
1771-1832

Sir Walter Scott, famous as an author of Scottish historical novels like *Ivanhoe* and *Rob Roy* has become one of Scotland's most famous sons. The Victorian gothic spire, The Scott Monument, completed in 1844, dominates Edinburgh's Princes Street. During his life he was a great dog lover and there are several portraits of him with his beloved dogs.

He was also intrigued by cats, as he observed to his friend and American author Washington Irving *'Ah! Cats are mysterious folk. There is more passing in their minds than we are aware of. It comes no doubt from their being so familiar with warlocks and witches'*. It was from a German fairy tale that Scott named his tabby cat Hinse of Hinsefeldt. There is a painting depicting Scott with his tomcat lying on his desk, painted by Sir John Watson Gordon eight years after Scott's death circa 1840. It can be seen at

http://www.walterscott.lib.ed.ac.uk/portraits/paintings/gordoncastlest.html.

You can also see one of Scott's dogs in this painting. There were several dogs throughout his life. His favourite, Maida, appears with him on The Scott Monument. The enmity between cats and dogs is legendary and it proved fatal in the case of Hinse and a bloodhound called Nimrod. It seems that Hinse ran out of lives and Nimrod out of patience at being tormented by Hinse and he struck a fatal blow in 1826.

ROBERT SOUTHEY *Poet*
1774-1843

The name Southey does not trip easily off the tongue in the same way that Wordsworth or Coleridge does. So, it's surprising to discover that they were all contemporaries. Southey's home, Greta Hall in Keswick, was a gathering place for such luminaries as Byron, Shelley and Keats. This gathering of some of the finest Romantic poets of their generation is perhaps understandable when we discover that Robert Southey was in fact Poet Laureate for thirty years. He was also a great lover of cats and Greta Hall was home to many of them over the years. In his correspondence to his family and friends he illustrated this love with many references to his beloved cats. These can be found in *The Life and Correspondence of Robert Southey* (1850), written by his son, Charles.

Southey had a fondness for giving his cats very grand and long names as witnessed in his letter to his friend, Grosvenor Bedford. On the death of Rumpel, he wrote that his full titles were:

The Most Noble the Archduke Rumpelstiltzchen, Marquis Macbum, Earl Tomlemagne, Baron Raticide, Waowhler, and Skaratch.

As well as being a prolific writer of poetry and prose, Southey also kept up a vast correspondence. The six volumes of his letters can be viewed at https://bit.ly/3n9ZfV5.

Greta Hall in Main Street, Keswick, which was also Coleridge's home, is now a bed and breakfast hotel. Its history and images can be viewed at

https://www.visitcumbria.com/cm/greta-hall/

LORD GEORGE GORDON BYRON, *Poet*
1788-1824

The popular image and perception of the poet Lord Bryon is one of a charismatic and passionate figure. He has been described as a rock star of his generation. There is no doubt that he was also eccentric and passionate about his love for all animals. During his time as a student at Cambridge University he was so incensed that pet dogs were banned, he bought a tame bear and used to parade him around the grounds on a chain. As there was no ban on bears in the rules the University could not forbid him.

According to his lifelong friend and fellow poet Percy Shelley, Byron's menagerie at his Venice palazzo consisted of ten horses, eight dogs, three monkeys, five cats, an eagle, a crow, a falcon, five peacocks, two guinea hens and an Egyptian crane. All the animals, apart from the horses, could roam freely about the house. One of his cats, Beppo, was said to drink milk from a skull. The cat may have been named by Byron after a male character in the epic poem he wrote in 1817 called *Beppo: A Venetian* Story which was a precursor to his most famous poem *Don Juan.* An eccentric and somewhat controversial figure during his lifetime, there is no doubting George Gordon Byron's love for all animals.

Chapter 6 – 19th Century

ALEXANDRE DUMAS, *Author,*
1802-1870

The Count of Monte Cristo and *The Three Musketeers,* two of Alexandre Dumas' most famous novels, have been translated into more than 100 languages and are the source of a multitude of films and television series.

When Napoleon was elected in 1851 Dumas fled to Brussels to escape not just the new regime but also his creditors. During this latter period of his literary life, in 1854, he published a newspaper, *Le Mousquetaire.* He wrote 28 columns called *Histoires de mes bêtes* (History of My Animals) and this is how we know about his love of cats. He recalls that whilst living with his mother and before his literary career began, they had a

29

cat called Mysouff. Dumas tells us that the cat acted more like a dog. Every morning he would escort Dumas to the Rue de Vaugirard and every evening wait for him at the same place. Mysouff required the door to be open and if this did not happen, he scratched persistently at the door until it was opened. Curiously, Dumas recounts that when he was delayed Mysouff did not stray from his cushion at the appointed time, somehow knowing that his master would not require his services on that particular evening. His second cat, called Mysouff II was found by Dumas' cook, Madame Lamargue abandoned behind a pile of wood in the cellar. He adopted him but was wary, as by this time he had collected an extensive collection of rare and exotic birds. Dumas also kept monkeys and one morning it was discovered that the monkeys had gnawed a hole into the aviary. Whilst some of the birds had flown away, the remainder had been killed and eaten by Mysouff II. The cat was locked in the aviary and fed a diet of bread and water and put on 'trial' by Dumas and his friends.

Mysouff II was 'declared guilty of complicity in the assassination of the doves and quails, also of the wrynecks, widow-birds, Indian sparrows, and other rare birds, but with extenuating circumstances. He was merely condemned to five years of incarceration with the apes.' Fortunately for Mysouff II, Dumas fell into financial difficulties shortly after 'sentence' was passed and he had to sell the monkeys. Mysouff II was liberated from his uncomfortable incarceration. The English translation by Alfred Allinson of *Histoires de mes bêtes* was published in 1909. These charming stories and others about Dumas' pets can be accessed at http://archive.org/details/mypetspets00dumarich.

This love of animals, and especially stray cats, prompted Dumas to form a Feline Defence League in the 1880s together with other famous writers like Baudelaire and Guy de Maupassant. On his death, in 1870, he was buried in his birthplace, Villers-Cotterêts. In 2002, for the bicentennial of his birth, President Jacques Chirac decided to re-inter his ashes and have them placed in the grand mausoleum of Le Panthéon in Paris. A grand ceremony involved a live television broadcast with his new coffin, draped in blue velvet, processed through Paris flanked by four mounted Republican guards dressed as The Four Musketeers. At last he took his place amongst other famous French authors like his contemporary Victor Hugo and his contribution to French literature and culture was finally recognised.

VICTOR HUGO, *Author*
1802-1885

Victor Hugo dominated French literary life for over fifty years. Most people know him as the author of *Les Miserables*. He had many pet cats during his life, but his favourite was called Chanoine who lived with him at his Parisian residence at the Place des Vosges (then called Place Royale). A popular French writer with the pen name Chamfleury, who wrote a book about cats called *Les Chats,* visited Hugo at his apartment. He noted that he saw a huge cat reclining on a large red ottoman in the centre of the room. In a letter to a friend written during Hugo's travels to the Rhineland in 1839 and 1842 he informed him that the reason he called his favourite cat Chanoine was because of 'his indolence and idleness'. It was also perhaps due to his large size, as chanoine means canon in French. It is thought that Chanoine also inspired one of Hugo's famous sayings about cats that 'God made the cat to give man the pleasure of petting the tiger'.

As well as being a literary giant, Hugo also played a political role in the life of France and was elected to the National Assembly in 1848. When Napoleon III seized power in 1851, he left his beloved France and fled to Brussels and then Jersey before finally settling in Guernsey. He lived in exile for fifteen years until his return in 1870. It was in Guernsey that he wrote his famous epic novel *Les Miserables*, a book that he had been planning for at least twenty years. It was published in 1862, whilst Hugo was still in exile, and whilst criticised by the establishment, its mass appeal was overwhelming. Today, in Paris, you can visit his apartment in Place des Vosges where he lived with Chanoine https://en.parisinfo.com/paris-museum-monument/71077/Maison-de-Victor-Hugo and walk along Avenue Victor-Hugo. His home in Guernsey, Hauteville House, is open to the public details http://www.museums.gov.gg/hauteville

EDGAR ALLEN POE, *Author*
1809-1849

Edgar Allen Poe was born Edgar Poe in Boston, USA, in 1809. Along with his siblings, Poe was abandoned by his father in 1810 and his mother died the following year. He was taken in by John and Frances Allen of Richmond, Virginia. And so he became Edgar Allen Poe, although the Allen family did not formally adopt him. He left his foster family when he enlisted in the army at the age of 18. He failed as an army cadet at West Point and he decided to become a full-time writer. The name of Edgar Allen Poe is today synonymous with horror stories. The macabre, gothic short stories or tales have become his legacy.

During his life Poe was recognised mostly as a literary critic. He became the first American author to become more famous in Europe than America.

In 1843 Poe published a short story in *The Saturday Evening Post* called *The Black Cat*. Reading it one might assume that Poe didn't like cats as it contains scenes of violence towards Pluto (the black cat). On the contrary, Poe loved cats which might explain the end of the story when Pluto has the last meow! Poe's favourite cat was not black but tortoiseshell and called Catarina. This adored feline would sit on Poe's shoulder when he was writing. At that time Poe was an impoverished writer who was prone to excess drinking and gambling. There was therefore little comfort for his wife when she was dying of tuberculosis, except for Catarina, who would curl up on her bed to provide warmth in their cold house. Today, in Poe's home town of Richmond, Virginia there is a museum dedicated to his life and works https://www.poemuseum.org/.

In honour of Poe's love of cats, the museum adopted two black kittens who were discovered one day in the museum's garden. In homage to Poe himself and *The Black Cat*, they were named Edgar and Pluto. If you would like to read *The Black Cat* you can access it at http://www.online-literature.com/poe/24/

ABRAHAM LINCOLN, *US President*
1809-1865

The 16th President of the United States, Abraham Lincoln was born in Hodgeville Kentucky in the Western frontier in 1809. He presided over the American Civil War when North and South battled daily for four years until April 1865 when General Robert E. Lee surrendered to General Grant. Five days later, Abraham Lincoln was assassinated at Ford's Theatre in Washington DC. The assassin, John Wilkes Booth was found in Virginia twelve days later and, after refusing to surrender, was shot and killed.

Abraham Lincoln is often ranked as the best President of the United States by its citizens and many monuments and museums are dedicated to him. Famously known as the man who abolished slavery and preserved the Union, many will not know of Lincoln's love of cats. Lincoln was the first President to have pet cats living in the White House. At the beginning of his Presidency he was given two small kittens as a gift from Secretary of State William H. Seward. They were named Tabby and Dixie and President Lincoln would sometimes seat Tabby next to him at dinner and feed him from a gold fork. It seems that he would pick up a cat and 'talk' to it for half an hour. He once observed, no doubt in a moment of exasperation, that 'Dixie is smarter than my whole cabinet! And furthermore, she doesn't talk back!' The enjoyment President Lincoln derived from playing with cats and kittens especially, led to his wife Mary saying that his hobby was 'cats'. It is not known what happened to Tabby and Dixie after Lincoln's assassination, but we do know that during his time at the White House they gave him great comfort and pleasure amidst the ravages of the American Civil War.

CHARLES DICKENS, *Author*
1812-1870

For many, Charles Dickens is the greatest novelist of the Victorian age. The Victorians loved his novels as much as we do today and his popularity, both in his lifetime and beyond, has never wavered. Although he travelled extensively abroad, his domestic life, when he was at home was filled with ten children and several cats. His famous quote 'What greater gift than the love of a cat?' shows how much he loved them. One of his favourites, Williamina was originally given to Dickens' daughter Mamie but, in her book, written about her father, she recounts that Williamina favoured her father.

The white cat was originally named William (after Shakespeare) but quickly renamed after (s)he produced a litter of kittens which she lovingly presented to Dickens in his study. One of Williamina's kittens remained at Gad's Hill in Kent, his country home. The kitten was deaf and wasn't named except the servants called him 'The Master's Cat' due to his devotion to Dickens.

The cat was always by his side as illustrated in this anecdote which Mamie recounts her father telling the family at breakfast.

The previous evening, he had been reading with the cat in the drawing room by candlelight. The candle suddenly went out, so he re-lit it and carried on reading. Dickens noticed the candle getting low again and looked up to see the cat deliberately put out the candle with his paw. As a way of getting attention this certainly did the trick and he got the petting and strokes he demanded. It appears that somewhere along the line this favoured cat was named Bob, maybe after Bob Cratchit in *A Christmas Carol.*

The fashion for taxidermy was popular in the 19th century and after Bob's death Dickens had his paw stuffed and made into a letter opener. The inscription on the handle of the letter opener reads 'C.D. In Memory of Bob 1862' This wasn't unusual at the time, although it seems rather macabre to us now. It did mean that he was still able to touch and feel the cat's paw every day and remember him. Maybe not so strange after all.

Today the letter opener is owned by the Berg Collection and housed at The New York Public Library. It was shown as part of the library's 2011 centennial exhibition to celebrate Dickens' 100th anniversary.

Click on @ https://bit.ly/33emxPQ to see a photo. The biography of Mamie Dickens called *My Father As I Recall Him* can be accessed at http://www.dickenslit.com/my-father-as-i-recall-him/myfatherdickens.html

CHARLOTTE BRONTË (1816-1855); EMILY BRONTË (1818-1848); ANNE BRONTË (1820-1849), *Authors*

The authors of such well-known classics *Jane Eyre*, *Wuthering Heights* and *Agnes Grey*, the Brontë sisters were well-known animal lovers. We know of two cats who the sisters doted on called Tom and Tiger. Tiger was a tabby cat and features in a painting by Emily alongside their dogs Keeper and Flossie. Ellen Nussey, a lifelong friend and correspondent of Charlotte's was a frequent visitor to the Haworth Parsonage. She tells us of another much loved cat called Black Tom, who according to Ellen, was everybody's favourite. She notes that 'It received such gentle treatment it seemed to have lost its cat's nature and subsided into luxurious amiability and contentment.' In an essay written by Emily in 1842 called *The Cat* she begins by telling us 'I can say with sincerity that I like cats; also I can give very good reasons why those who despise them are wrong.'

This short, charming essay can be read at http://kleurrijkbrontesisters.blogspot.com/2010/07/title-cat-author-emily-bronte.html Emily and Anne particularly loved animals and their diary papers reference their many pets, including Tom and Tiger. A rare page from Emily's diary paper of 1845 with an illustration of her room with Flossy and Keeper and a cat curled up on the bed can be seen at http://kleurrijkbrontesisters.blogspot.com/2014/02/diary-paper-sketch-of-emily-with-her.html

QUEEN VICTORIA
1819-1901

It is well known that our current Royal Family like dogs as pets rather than cats. Because of Queen Victoria, cats were finally brought in from the cold of the 19th century streets to the warmth of the hearth. As a child, her main companions were animals and dolls. In 1840 she gave her Royal patronage to what became the Royal Society for the Prevention of Cruelty to Animals (or RSPCA as it is now more commonly called). The Queen commissioned many portraits of her pets and her love of cats can be seen in the charming painting called *Cat and Dogs Belonging to the Queen,* painted in 1885 by

Charles Burton Barber. Featuring three of her dogs looking up at a pretty tabby kitten sitting on a chair, it is part of The Royal Collection and can be seen at https://www.rct.uk/collection/search#/1/collection/403 567/cat-and-dogs-belonging-to-queen-victoria. It currently hangs in the Horn Room at Osborne House on the Isle of Wight. Although not in this picture, Queen Victoria particularly liked a pair of Blue Persians.

First Cat Show 1871 in London, England

Her love of cats is further confirmed by her insistence that a cat be included in the picture on her RSPCA Queen's Medal of Kindness, a fact noted in a letter sent to *The Spectator* shortly after her death. In the anonymous letter the writer notes 'During these latter days I have observed several times, and notably once in The Spectator, the statement that our late good Queen did not like cats.' The letter explains that according to the last RSPCA annual report, by command of the Queen, a cat was included in the picture on the medal. He concludes that 'In justice alike to the all-round humanity of Queen Victoria and to poor Pussy, I think that this little fact should be made better known.' Well, Sir or Madam, it is now. Towards the end of her life it is said that her favourite cat and one which outlived her, was an Angora called White Heather. The Queen's son, King Edward VII followed his mother's instructions and allowed her to continue living at Buckingham Palace for the rest of her life.

FLORENCE NIGHTINGALE, *Nurse, Social Reformer*
1820-1910

Florence Nightingale, named after the city of her birth, was called 'The Lady with the Lamp' by the soldiers she would visit on her rounds during the 19th century Crimean War. She was a pioneer in terms of hygiene, patient care and nursing methods during this time. The conditions in the makeshift field hospital were appalling, not least because of the rats. This problem was solved when a soldier presented a yellow cat to control the vermin. Florence must have developed feelings for the cat as it was shipped back to England after the war but unfortunately it died in transit. The super-human efforts of Florence during the Crimean War left her with a legacy of ill-health for the rest of her life, which was a long one, as she died in 1910 at the age of 90. It is believed that she contracted brucellosis from infected goat milk. For the last twenty years of her life she was bed-ridden. Despite her ill-health she was very productive and worked to reform conditions in India, in the London workhouses, and for the British military.

As the founder of modern-day nursing she wrote books and pamphlets and was an authority on hospital planning. She came from a wealthy family and post-war she lived in the Burlington Hotel where her constant companions during her adult life also resided. These were her beloved cats. She is believed to have owned more than 60 in her lifetime. Whilst at the hotel she was given a family of Persian cats. There were at least six of them and they wandered around at will causing mischief. They would upset her ink and make paw prints in her correspondence.

The cats gave her immense pleasure but not so for her servants who were tasked with preparing special meals and generally taking care of them. She was particularly fond of a large Persian called Mr. Bismarck. Her staff were given detailed instructions about his mealtimes and told that he was 'particularly partial to a little rice pudding with his 5 o'clock tea'. Meals for the cats were served to an exact schedule on china plates in her room. On a rare excursion to see her sister, a Persian kitten Quiz was the source of a great deal of alarm when she went missing. During a train journey, Quiz was in her basket on Florence's knee when she suddenly leapt out of the window and onto the track and disappeared. Not afraid of using her fame, in dramatic fashion Florence summoned the help of all the stationmasters in England to find Quiz. The mischievous kitten was found by the Watford stationmaster, injured but alive. The kitten was sent to Euston station where she spent the night in the parcels office before being re-united with her relieved owner. That Florence should go to so much trouble was typical of her love and care for her cats. Much of the domestic detail of Florence's life with her cats is from her prolific correspondence. You can still see the paw prints of many of her cats on her letters. The Nightingale Collection of writings is one of the largest in the British Library. They have been digitised and can be accessed in their original format at http://hgar-srv3.bu.edu/web/florence-nightingale/home. Florence chose cats for company over any other companions because she believed that they possessed more sympathy and feeling than human beings. Maybe, after seeing some of the worst excesses of human nature during the Crimean War, she preferred to shower her love and affection on these most charming animals who offered her unconditional love in return.

MARK TWAIN *Author*
1835-1910

In the family home of Samuel Langhorne Clemens, cats were the preferred choice of pet. In fact, growing up, Samuel was surrounded by at least nineteen cats, loved by his mother for their independence. Samuel wrote under many pseudonyms but finally settled on Mark Twain as his literary alter-ego. As well as being a famous author for such books as *Adventures of*

Huckleberry Finn and *The Adventures of Tom Sawyer,* Twain maintained his family's tradition of loving cats. His daughter Susie observed 'The difference between Papa and Momma is that Momma loves morals and Papa loves cats.' He had many cats during his lifetime and chose eccentric names for them. These include Apollinaris, Beelzebub, Blatherskite, Tammany and Zoroaster. Twain explained that the reason for their complicated names was so that his children could practice the pronunciation of large and difficult words. He described how he liked to 'cram' a kitten into one of the corner pockets of a billiard table so that the game was obstructed and the kitten could watch the game. It would often put out its paw and divert a passing ball. His dedication to his cats was legendary and when Bambino (a gift from his daughter Clara) went missing he put an advert in the *New York American* newspaper offering a $5 reward for his return. Although it seems that many people turned up at his door with all sorts of cats, Bambino came home on his own.

Another of Twain's eccentricities was that whenever he travelled, he would rent kittens to make the place of his own. He would always leave money behind for their care. Although originally written in 1880, it wasn't until 1959 with the posthumous publication of two stories about cats that we see Twain combine his two great loves, his family and cats. The book is called

Concerning Cats and the stories are *A Cat Tale* and *The Autobiography of Belshazzar*. In the introduction to *A Cat Tale*, Twain explained that his two small daughters, Susie and Clara wanted him to tell them original bedtime stories and, 'I thought maybe other little people might like to try one of my narcotics – so I offer this one.' Of the many quotes attributed to Mark Twain about his love of cats, I think this one sums up his and perhaps every cat lover's fascination with our feline friends. 'I simply can't resist a cat, particularly a purring one. They are the cleanest, cunningest, and most intelligent things I know, outside of the girl you love, of course'.

Mark Twain, his wife Olivia and their three daughters spent 30 years in a house that he built in Hartford, Connecticut, where many of their beloved cats would have lived. It is now a museum and open to visitors. Details can be found at
https://marktwainhouse.org/

THOMAS HARDY *Author*
1840-1928

Thomas Hardy, known for his novels about tragic heroines and the twists and turns of fate, was very fond of cats. Although his novels made him famous and wealthy, he viewed himself as a poet primarily and his poem *Last Words to a Dumb Friend* express his grief at the loss of his cat. It is not clear which cat Hardy is referring to. In the pet cemetery at his house, Max Gate in Dorset, he buried assorted cats and dogs. Trot and Cobby are known to have belonged to Hardy. Trot, especially, was much-loved with Hardy apparently calling him Kiddleywinkempoops. Whilst this may seem eccentric, what cat owner hasn't or doesn't succumb to affectionate nonsensical name calling from time to time. Whilst Trot was obviously adored, Cobby (a blue Persian) on the other hand, if the story is to be believed, perhaps took the love of his master a step too far. It is true, that after Hardy's death in 1926 the cat disappeared. The apparent explanation for this is macabre and somewhat incredulous. Hardy had instructed that his heart should be buried in the village of Stinsford and his ashes laid to rest in Poets Corner in Westminster Abbey. After the heart was removed, it was wrapped in a tea towel and put into a biscuit tin in readiness for the undertaker. On his arrival, the undertaker only found a few remains of the heart and a well-fed Cobby. The undertaker then decided that the only action to be taken was to indeed bury Hardy's heart, which was now apparently inside the cat. In this macabre twist, and fitting of a Hardy novel, Cobby met his fate and was put into Hardy's casket and buried. In other versions of the story Cobby was spared and a substitute heart was buried. In 1996, the journalist Frank Smyth wrote an article about this macabre incident. Intrigued by the story he thoroughly researched it and his findings can be read at https://westdorsetconfidential.wordpress.com/2012/10/16/ardys-eart-and-the-hungry-cat/

There is little definitive evidence that this 'myth' is true, but it does seem ironic and strangely fitting that the themes of tragedy and fate, so central to Hardy's novels, are present in this story. Hardy's house, Max Gate in Dorchester is now a National Trust property and visitors can also see Hardy's pet cemetery with many of the gravestones engraved by him personally. https://www.nationaltrust.org.uk/max-gate

Last Words to a Dumb Friend by Thomas Hardy

Pet was never mourned as you,
Purrer of the spotless hue,
Plumy tail, and wistful gaze
While you humoured our queer ways,
Or outshrilled your morning call
Up the stairs and through the hall -
Foot suspended in its fall -
While, expectant, you would stand
Arched, to meet the stroking hand;
Till your way you chose to wend
Yonder, to your tragic end.

Never another pet for me!
Let your place all vacant be;
Better blankness day by day
Than companion torn away.

Better bid his memory fade,
Better blot each mark he made,
Selfishly escape distress
By contrived forgetfulness,
Than preserve his prints to make
Every morn and eve an ache.

From the chair whereon he sat
Sweep his fur, nor wince thereat;
Rake his little pathways out
Mid the bushes roundabout;
Smooth away his talons' mark
From the claw-worn pine-tree bark,
Where he climbed as dusk embrowned,
Waiting us who loitered round.

Strange it is this speechless thing,
Subject to our mastering,
Subject for his life and food
To our gift, and time, and mood;
Timid pensioner of us Powers,
His existence ruled by ours,
Should - by crossing at a breath
Into safe and shielded death,
By the merely taking hence
Of his insignificance -
Loom as largened to the sense,

Shape as part, above man's will,
Of the Imperturbable.

As a prisoner, flight debarred,
Exercising in a yard,
Still retain I, troubled, shaken,
Mean estate, by him forsaken;
And this home, which scarcely took
Impress from his little look,
By his faring to the Dim
Grows all eloquent of him.

Housemate, I can think you still
Bounding to the window-sill,
Over which I vaguely see
Your small mound beneath the tree,
Showing in the autumn shade
That you moulder where you played

THEODORE ROOSEVELT, *US President*
1858-1919

The assassination of President William McKinley in 1901 meant that Theodore (Teddy) Roosevelt, as his Vice President, became the 26th President of the United States. At 42, he remains the youngest man to become President. He moved his family of six children and enormous menagerie into the White House where they lived for the next eight years. During this time, they had 9 dogs, a garter snake, a pony, a pig,a badger, a rat and guinea pigs as well as a hen, macaw and rooster. They also owned two cats, Slippers and Tom Quartz. In 1903 in a letter to his son Kermit, who was at boarding school, Roosevelt described Tom Quartz as 'the cunningest kitten I ever seen'. He then describes to Kermit how the kitten has tormented Jack, Kermit's terrier, by leaping at him and hanging onto his legs. In the same letter he recalls how Tom Quartz also leapt at Mr. Cannon, the Speaker of the House, as he was coming down the stairs.

Whilst it seems that Tom Quartz (named after the cat in Mark Twain's book *Roughing It*) was up to all sorts of mischief, Slippers, their grey six-toed pet cat, was much more relaxed and easy going. In fact, she once fell asleep in a hallway of the White House in the middle of the route of honoured guests to a State banquet. Instead of disturbing her, Roosevelt guided his guests around the sleeping cat, no doubt causing much bemusement to his guests. In 1919 Roosevelt published a book called *Letters to His Children*. You can read more stories about the Roosevelt family and their pets at
http://www.gutenberg.org/files/6467/6467-h/6467-h.htm

COLETTE, *Author*
1873-1954
Sidonie-Gabrielle Colette was a famous French author and woman of letters nominated for the Nobel Prize in Literature in 1948. She was also known as a mime, actress, and journalist. She was a prolific writer of over 50 novels, her most famous being *Gigi*, written in 1944. This was made into an acclaimed Hollywood film,

directed by Vincent Minelli and starring Leslie Caron and Maurice Chevalier. It won the 1959 Oscar for Best Picture. In January 2019 a feature film *Colette* starring Keira Knightly was released. The film details her relationship with her first husband and her introduction to Parisian avant-garde society in the late 1800s. Colette's passion for cats didn't begin until 1926 when she bought a pearl grey Chartreux cat at a market. Her lifelong love of cats, and dogs also, inspired her. Her pearl gray cat La Chatte was the inspiration for her slim novel *La Chatte* which she wrote in 1933. The novel has three characters, husband, wife and Saha, the cat, who belongs to the husband. Eventually the husband's love for his cat leads to the breakdown of his marriage after the wife attempts to kill Saha by throwing her off the balcony. The cat survives and the husband leaves his wife and takes the cat. Colette's second husband complained that, 'When I enter a room where you're alone with animals I feel I'm being indiscreet'. However busy she was she believed that 'time spent with cats is never wasted'. Colette's favourite dogs were French Bulldogs. She wrote that she believed that 'our perfect companions never have fewer than four feet'. When she died, in 1954, she was the first woman in France to be given a state funeral. She is buried in Père Lachaise in Paris.

SIR ERNEST SHACKLETON, *Antarctic Explorer*
1874-1922

When *The Endurance* set sail on 1ˢᵗ August 1914 from
London's East India Docks on its Trans-Antarctica
expedition, its crew was joined by a tiger-striped tabby
cat. The handsome cat had been found by the ship's
carpenter Harry McNeish, sleeping in one of his
toolboxes before departure. Ship's cats were popular
and useful, they caught vermin and kept the crew's food
supplies free from rats and mice. The cat was named
Mrs. Chippy after the English nickname for a carpenter.
Even when it was discovered that Mrs. was a Mr., the
crew did not change his name because they felt that he
behaved like a possessive wife towards McNeish,

following him around the ship. Mrs. Chippy became very popular with the crew and was an efficient mouser. They were impressed by his ability to walk along the inch-wide rails of the ships in the most treacherous seas. After many months trapped by the Antarctic ice, *The Endurance* finally started to break up and on October 27th 1915, the crew and Mrs. Chippy were ordered to 'abandon ship'. The crew, Mrs. Chippy and several dogs were stranded on the polar ice. The prospect of having to walk a great distance across the Antarctic in order to reach land forced Shackleton to make the decision that Mrs. Chippy and three puppies had to be shot. A rather unusual account of what happened on 29th October 1915 can be read in *Mrs. Chippy's Last Expedition* by Caroline Alexander, published by Bloomsbury. The book is written from Mrs. Chippy's perspective. It is filled with illustrations by W.E. How who served on The Endurance, and photographs by Frank Hurley. This charming account, based on fact, recounts that on that fateful day the crew came to say goodbye and that Mrs. Chippy enjoyed a bowl of sardines and then fell asleep. The crew of The Endurance did eventually reach South Georgia in May 1916. McNeish never forgave Shackleton for shooting his beloved Mrs. Chippy and the acrimony between them resulted in McNeish not receiving a Polar Medal. This is despite McNeish playing a vital role in the crew's survival, ensuring their lifeboats were fit for purpose. This is not the end of the story: when McNeish finally gave up the sea he worked and lived on the waterfront in Wellington, New Zealand. On his death in 1930 he was given a funeral with full naval honours, although he was destitute and buried in a pauper's grave. At last, in 1959 a headstone was raised by the New Zealand Antarctic Society. Finally, in 2004 a bronze life-sized sculpture of Mrs. Chippy was placed on his grave – Master and his cat reunited. The grave, together with the sculpture can be seen in Karori Cemetery, Wellington.

The story of McNish and Mrs. Chippy is one of legend as it continues to intrigue and enchant down the generations. In 1998 McNeish had an island in South

Georgia named after him and in 2011, the only known photograph of Mrs. Chippy perching on Perce Blackborow's shoulder was issued as a stamp by South Georgia. It was part of a set of six stamps to commemorate animals associated with the island.

SIR WINSTON CHURCHILL, *Prime Minister* 1874-1965

Winston Churchill has one of the most recognised faces in the world. He topped a television poll in 2002 when UK viewers voted for their 100 Greatest Britons and is probably our most popular Prime Minister. I imagine most people would connect Churchill with dogs, particularly bulldogs. As a teen in 1851 he apparently sold his bicycle to buy a bulldog called Dodo and during his lifetime he was often called 'The British Bulldog'.

He was in fact a lover of all animals and, surprisingly perhaps, extremely fond of cats. During his childhood he was surrounded by a menagerie which included pigs, fish, butterflies, sheep, horses and black swans. In his adult life cats were present at his official residences as well as at his family home, Chartwell, in Kent. During his war-time Premiership living at No.10, he had a large grey cat called Nelson. He was named after the great Admiral because Churchill thought him the bravest cat he had ever known after seeing him chase a huge dog out of the Admiralty. The cat was well named: after Churchill moved into No.10 in May 1940, Nelson challenged the resident cat, Munich Mouser. This cat was left behind after Neville Chamberlain's defeat and rather cheekily named by the Churchill family. Sadly, like his master, he was unceremoniously chased out of No.10 by Nelson who could stroll freely along the corridors of power and could often be found asleep in the Cabinet Room. Whilst Nelson may have been top cat downstairs at No.10, it was another grey, Smokey who reigned supreme in the Churchills' private residence above No. 10. He kept Clementine Churchill company during her husband's absences, although she also had a Siamese cat called Gabriel who was resident at Chartwell. Another feline friend was a stray kitten taken in by staff at No.10. He jumped up onto Winston Churchill's lap whilst he was listening to a wireless report of his successful speech at the Conservative Party Conference. The kitten was named Margate because the Conference that year took place in Margate. Churchill loved all cats, but marmalade cats were a particular favourite. It has been reported that during some of the worst times of World War 2 his marmalade cat Tango proved a welcome distraction. At lunch he would sit beside Churchill and, despite having the future of Europe on his mind, he would converse with Tango, wipe his eyes and apologise that rationing meant he couldn't have cream. It is Jock, his last marmalade cat, who gave Churchill much comfort in his old age. When the Churchill family handed over Chartwell to The National Trust in 1965, Churchill's great affection for Jock was recognised. They stipulated that there should always be a marmalade cat with a white bib and four white socks called Jock in residence at the family home. The current resident is Jock VII who arrived at Chartwell in May 2020 as a six-month rescue kitten. You can read about this latest arrival and see pictures of him at

https://www.nationaltrust.org.uk/chartwell/features/jock-vii-of-chartwell

PAUL KLEE, *Artist*
1879-1940

Of all the artists working in the 20th century, Paul Klee is perhaps the most devoted to the study and painting of cats. The inspiration for as many as 28 paintings, was his beloved white long-haired Bimbo II. Klee was born in Berne, Switzerland but spent a large part of his adult life in Germany. He studied art at The Academy of Fine Arts in Munich before being called up by the German army to fight in World War I. In 1920 he worked alongside Wassily Kandinsky as a teacher at the German Bauhaus. Klee's art was heavily influenced by the modern art movements of the day. His style was innovative and difficult to categorise, although the Nazis labelled it 'degenerate'. Alongside other artists, Klee fled to Switzerland. Throughout this period, he had the companionship of cats. His cats Fritzi, a mackerel tabby, and Bimbo I were with him during the 1920s and he took Bimbo II to Switzerland. As observed by the American art critic, Edward M.M.Warburg, Klee would let Bimbo II wander over his paintings leaving paw prints and laughed that 'Many years from now, one of your art connoisseurs will wonder how in the world I ever got that effect'. Of the 9,000 paintings he left after his death, many of them show a cat in the corner or on a floating table. One of the most familiar paintings of a cat by Klee is *Cat and*

Bird, painted in 1928 and owned by the Museum of Modern Art in New York. You can view the painting at http://www.moma.org/collection/object.php?object_id =79456.

ALBERT EINSTEIN, *Physicist*
1879-1955
Albert Einstein is best-known for his general theory of relativity. He was awarded the Nobel Prize for Physics in 1921. Born in Germany in 1879, he moved to Switzerland in 1895 to finish his schooling. At the age of 17 he renounced his German citizenship to avoid

military service. He emigrated to America in 1933 and took up a position at the Institute for Advanced Study at Princeton in New Jersey. During his years at the Institute he kept a tom cat called Tiger. Einstein believed that Tiger became depressed and melancholic when it rained. Ernst Strauss, his assistant, recalls Einstein saying to the cat, 'I know what's wrong, dear fellow, but I don't know how to turn it off'. Maybe it was Einstein's observation of Tiger's behaviour that prompted him to note 'A man has to work so hard so that something of his personality stays alive. A tomcat has it so easy, he has only to spray and his presence is there for years on rainy days'. In trying to describe in layman's terms how radio worked, Einstein used the analogy of 'a very, very long cat. You pull his tail in New York and his head is meowing in Los Angeles. Do you understand this? And radio operates exactly the same way: you send signals here; they receive them there. The only difference is that there is no cat.' Cordula, a grey cat, was adopted by Einstein in 1935, having rescued her as a kitten from a tree whilst shopping for groceries. He spoke to her in German and the cat endeared herself to him by responding to his native language and he took her home. Einstein called her Cordula, which is a German name derived from the Latin word for heart. Einstein's wife, Elsa had been diagnosed with heart and kidney problems, so perhaps

Einstein thought the kitten was a good omen. Cordula became a much-loved pet and would respond to German phrases and chase balls like a dog. After the death of his wife in 1936, Cordula no doubt gave him comfort. The consolation that Cordula gave him and his love of music are no doubt the inspirations behind his statement that 'the only escape from the miseries of life are music and cats'. Cordula became his constant companion after the death of his wife. When he received his American citizenship in 1940, he is said to have remarked to her 'Cordula, I am an American now. You have always been American but have adopted my German language. I am grateful for you.' His faithful cat lived until 1949, fourteen years after she was rescued from a tree, finally succumbing to kidney failure with her devoted owner by her side.

PABLO PICASSO, *Artist*
1881-1973

Whilst Picasso never had a specific Cat Period, like his famous Blue and Rose Periods, he was inspired by cats and incorporated them into several paintings, famously *Dora Maar au Chat* (1941) but also *Cat and Crab on the Beach* (1965), *Lobster and Cat* (1965), and *Cat Seizing a Bird* (1939), as well as using them as motifs on some of his ceramics and sculptures. We know he had at least one cat, a Siamese called Minou who lived with him in Montmarte when he was a struggling artist. The fictionalised story of Minou and Picasso was the subject of a children's book, *Picasso and Minou* (2008) by P. I. Maltbie.

T S ELIOT, *Poet*
1888-1965

T.S. Eliot was arguably the most important English-language poet of the 20th century. Thomas Stearns Eliot was born in St. Louis, Missouri in 1888 and became a British citizen in 1927. His seminal metaphysical poem *The Waste Land* is a central work of modernist poetry, and he won the Nobel Prize for Literature in 1948. It is curious therefore that someone of Eliot's literary stature should have produced a light-hearted collection of poems called *Old Possum's Book of Practical Cats*. Old Possum was a nickname given to him by Ezra Pound, a fellow American expatriate poet. Eliot originally wrote the poems in letters to his godchildren. The first edition has a cover illustration drawn by Eliot of himself at the top of a wall, a ladder lent against the wall which a group of cats are climbing up. The names of the cats in Eliot's collection are now well known because of the Andrew Lloyd Webber musical *Cats,* which was based on the book and has been an international success. Macavity The Mystery Cat, Jellicles, Grizabella, Rum Tum Tigger and Mr. Mistoffelees are now all familiar cat names. The names of Eliot's own cats George Pushdragon, Jellylorum, Mirza Murad Alibeg, Cockalorum, The Musical Box, Noilly Prat, Pattipaws, Tantomile and Wiscus demonstrate his original and imaginative literary mind. Eliot took the naming of cats seriously as he explains in his poem 'The Naming of Cats' which can be accessed at

http://famouspoetsandpoems.com/poets/t_s_eliot/poems/15121

His love of cats both fictional and real reveals a facet of Eliot's personality not immediately obvious to readers of his more serious literary works. The popularity of the musical *Cats* does mean that *Old Possum's Book of Practical Cats* is the collection of poems for which he is best known.

70

PAUL GALLICO, *Author*
1897-1976

Paul Gallico was a famous American sportswriter in the 1920s and 30s before he turned his attention and talent to novels and short stories. The work for which he was most associated with, due to their film adaptations in the 1970s, are *The Snow Goose*, and *The Poseidon Adventure*. Years before his success, his love of cats led him to write several novels and stories about them. Whilst the names of his own personal cats are not well known, the names he gave his fictional cats, Jennie and Thomasina in particular, are known to many of the readers of these classic American children's books. No doubt it was his fascination with cats that inspired him to write *Jennie* in 1950. Originally titled *The Abandoned* in America, *Jennie* is written from the cat's perspective, a theme he continued in his 1964 book *The Silent Miaow*. This is an 'instructional' manual written by a cat or 'translated from the feline'. It 'instructs' fellow cats in how to manipulate and dominate their adoptive household and train them so that they understand and cater for your every need. It is considered a classic 'cat psychology' book by many cat lovers and is still in print. In 1957 *Thomasina: The Cat Who Thought She Was God* was published and in 1964 Walt Disney Studios released it as a film called *The Three Lives of Thomasina*. In 1972, four years before his death, he published *Honourable Cat*, a book of 60 cat poems with colour photographs. In 1968 a teacher wrote to him and explained she had used some of his books to inspire reluctant readers and they had been of great use. In his letter of reply he wrote that of all his books (of which there were many) his preferred favourites were *The Abandoned* (published as *Jennie* in the UK) and Thomasina. Gallico was a prolific writer, he wrote over forty books on a wide range of subjects. He left America in the late 1930s and lived mostly in Europe, including London. In the latter years of his life he lived in Antibes, where he died aged 79.

BEVERLEY NICHOLS, *Author*
1898-1983

Beverley Nichols was an English author who wrote about subjects as diverse as politics and detective novels. He was certainly prolific as he wrote more than 60 novels and plays. He is probably best remembered for his books on gardening and his weekly columns in *Woman's Own* which he wrote for over twenty years. He wrote two books on cats, *Cats ABC* and its companion *Cats XYZ* which featured his cats Four, Five and Oscar who lived with him post-World War 2. Nichols didn't like to use the phrase 'cat-lover', instead he categorised people as 'F' or 'Non-F' signifying feline or non-feline by their natural inclination. It seems that his favourite breed of cat was the Siamese as cats One to Seven were all from the same breed. His black cat Oscar was also known as Eight . One of Nichols' many quotes about cats sums up why the majority of 'F's' are drawn to the cheeky and mischievous nature of our feline friends as he explains that 'most of us rather like our cats to have a streak of wickedness. I should not feel quite easy in the company of any cat that walked about the house with a saintly expression.' Whilst his Siamese cats were certainly named as numbers, he omitted the number six as he explained that he thought it sounded like 'sicks' – not a very palatable name when calling the cat to dinner!

ERNEST HEMINGWAY, *Author*
1899-1961

For many visitors to the Florida Keys, the home of Ernest Hemingway in Key West is a must-see destination. The house, where he lived during the winters between 1931 and 1939 with his second wife Pauline, is now officially called the Ernest Hemingway Home and Museum. Whilst the opportunity to wander inside the house where Hemingway completed *A Farewell to Arms* is no doubt of interest, the main attraction are the 40-50 polydactyl cats who inhabit the property. These cats have six toes and it is believed are descended from a white polydactyl cat called Snow White given to Hemingway by a ship's captain, during his time at Key West. Hemingway's love of cats did not begin in Key West, for he had a cat called Feather K (short for Kitty) in Toronto and then F. Puss whilst he lived in Paris with his first wife Hadley. It is a myth that Hemingway lived with lots of cats in Key West, at least latterly. According to a 1972 *Los Angeles Times* article by Charles Hillinger, Hemingway's last wife and widow, Mary, states, 'Ernest... never kept animals at the Key West house during the last twenty years of his life. He never stayed at Key West long enough to bother with animals after his divorce from Pauline'. What is not in dispute is the fact that in his house in Cuba he did indeed surround himself and indulge his passion for cats. The hilltop farmhouse Finca Vigia (Lookout Farm) was rented by Hemingway and his third wife, journalist Martha Gellhorn in 1939. The finca's established cat community grew with the purchase of Tester, re-named Princessa because of her elegant nature, and a stray kitten called Dillinger, re-named Boise. The adoption of a half-Maltese kitten, Willy, completed Hemingway's Cuban cat community in his first year of residence. It appears that Princessa and Boise mated prodigiously and by the end of 1943 there were eleven house cats living with the couple. In his novel *Islands in the Stream* Hemingway immortalised three of the cats: Princessa, Boise and Goats (aka Bigotes and/or Friendless). They are companions to the main character, Thomas Hudson, and it is not difficult to imagine the dialogue between Hudson and the cats being directly drawn from Hemingway's own 'conversations' with these cats. By the time his fourth wife, Mary Welsh, joined him at the Finca in 1945, his cat family had grown to twenty-three cats (and five dogs). The principal cat family consisted of Princessa, Boise, Friendless, Friendless's Brother, Willy, Uncle Wolfer, Good Will, Fatso, Furhouse, Thruster, and Littless Kitty. Shortly after Mary's arrival, Thruster gave birth to three male kittens. For some reason Hemingway believed that cats liked the 's' sound in their names and with his typical indecision and liking for changing his cats' names he called one Stephen Spender, later changed to Spendthrift shortened to Spendy. His brother was firstly called Shakespeare, then Barbershop and finally Shopsky, whilst the third male was firstly and finally called Ecstasy. The house cats lived in splendour in a white tower he had specially built for them. They were a source of much happiness to Hemingway and Mary, who called them 'love sponges'. It is perhaps the fact that, as he remarked, 'a cat has absolute emotional honesty; human beings, for one reason or another, may hide their feelings, but a cat does not,' which made him grow to love and admire them. Hemingway's Cuban finca was his refuge during the winter for over twenty years. It was where he wrote the majority of *For Whom The Bell Tolls* and *Old Man and The Sea*. Shortly after leaving Cuba in 1960, after the Castro revolution, he bought a house in Ketchum, Idaho and it was there in 1961 that he killed himself. His Cuban finca, and all its contents became the property of the Cuban Government. The finca is situated 9 miles outside Havana in San Francisco de Paula. After years of neglect the Government restored it in 2007.

It has become The Hemingway Museum, details at http://www.hemingwaycuba.com/hemingway-house-cuba.html.

At https://www.themagazineantiques.com/article/ernest-hemingway-cuba-home/ there are photographs of the interior of Finca Vigia which hasn't changed since Hemingway departed and still has all of his possessions.

Chapter 7 – 20th Century

WILLIAM S. BURROUGHS, *Author*
1914-1997

William Burroughs is known as a major figure of the Beat Generation and also as a lover of cats in his later life. He surrounded himself with them, all strays, after he moved to Kansas in the 1980s. In his last recorded diary entry, he wrote '*The only thing can resolve conflict is love, like I felt for Fletch and Ruski, Spooner, and Calico. Pure love. What I feel for my cats, present and past. Love? What is it? Most natural painkiller what there is. LOVE.*' His most famous novel was *The Naked Lunch*, published in 1959. In 1986 he wrote an autobiographical novella called *The Cat Inside* where he wrote about his love of cats and how in particular little Ruski restored his humanity. It has been said that the grief he felt on the death of his favourite, Fletch, hastened Burroughs' own death just three weeks later.

HAROLD WILSON, *British Prime Minister*
1916-1995
Nemo, a British Siamese Sealpoint was the pet of Harold Wilson's family long before he first became Prime Minister in 1964. Naturally, he went with the family when they moved in No.10 Downing Street. He's pictured on official photographs of the family and Harold would even take Nemo into Cabinet Meetings and place him on his lap. Maybe stroking Nemo alleviated Harold's stress and anxiety during any

particularly tense moments. The Wilsons didn't want to be parted from their beloved cat even during holidays and used to take him with them to their holiday home in the Isles of Scilly.

DORIS LESSING *Author*
1919-2013

Doris May Lessing, the celebrated author, was born in Iran to British parents. They moved to Southern Rhodesia (now Zimbabwe) when she was six. At the age of thirty she moved to London and began to pursue a literary career. Doris Lessing has had a constant relationship with cats. Growing up in Rhodesia, now Zimbabwe, her feline love affair began with the semi-feral cats that roamed her family's farm. As well as her celebrated novels Doris has also published several charming and sweet books about cats and her relationships with them including *Doris Lessing On Cats* (2008) and *Particularly Cats* (1979), an evocative look at the cats Doris has lived with, illustrated by Anne Robinson. Her distinguished literary career included being shortlisted three times for the Booker Prize and culminated in being awarded the Nobel Prize for Literature in 2007.

SIR KINGSLEY AMIS, *Author*
1922-1995

'I associate a person having a cat with them being gentler than other people. Cats stimulate the fancy; we weave fantasies about them.'

Kingsley Amis loved the company of cats and said that he was enough of a cat-lover to be suspicious of a household that didn't have a cat. He said that his cat talks and you can understand her 'if you've a sympathetic ear'. His beautiful white longhaired cat Sarah Snow was the inspiration for the poem *Cat English* (1987). It was published in *The Listener* and *The Sunday Telegraph* in 1987 but didn't appear in any of his poetry collections.

ANDY WARHOL, *Artist*
1928-1987
Andy Warhol's signature style of repetition in his silk-screen prints of domestic products like the Campbell's

soup can and Brillo pad may have its origins in a rather unlikely place. In his early career, after his move to New York from Pittsburgh, his mother, Julia, arrived to live with him along with her two cats Hester and Sam. Other versions of this story are that Warhol was given Hester as a present from actress Gloria Swanson and thought she might be lonely so he acquired Sam. The two cats proceeded to produce several large litters of kittens, all Siamese. Warhol's answer to what he should call these cats was simple, he called them all Sam. We know this because in 1954, together with Julia, he produced a limited-edition book of hand-coloured lithographs called *25 Cats Name Sam and One Blue Pussy*. His mother, in charge of the hand-written calligraphy, omitted the 'd' in 'name' but Warhol didn't correct it. The book contained illustrations of the cats by Warhol and captions by his mother – but there were only 17 illustrations, not 25. To keep track of the cats, his mother also named them after colours, i.e. Red Sam, Yellow Sam etc. The book was a limited edition of 190 and was apparently produced so that Warhol could advertise the cats to his friends. He also used the books as a marketing tool, giving them to magazine art directors to show his skills. When Hester died in 1957 a second book called *Holy Cats* was produced, again in collaboration with his mother, showing cats in heaven. In the mid-60s Warhol moved his art studio to a building in East Manhattan called The Factory. It became a focal point for the avant-garde and also home to two cats called Black Lace and White Pussy. Warhol was evasive about his private life, few knew that he lived with his mother until her death in 1972. Whilst his love of cats and other animals was not widely known he did create a series of images called *Cats and Dogs* in 1976. In 1994 a book called *Cats, Cats, Cats* featuring many of his cat illustrations was published. The images are from the archives of The Andy Warhol Foundation for the Visual Arts and is still available. The children's book *Uncle Andy's Cats* (2009) was written and illustrated by Warhol's nephew, James Warhola. It tells the story of all the Sam cats and Warhol's love for his cats in general.

ANNE FRANK, *Diarist*
1929-1945

Many personal possessions had to be left behind when the Frank family went into hiding in the loft of a warehouse in Amsterdam in 1942. The sadness at leaving favourite toys and books could not match the way that Anne felt about leaving her beloved cat Moortje. When the Franks moved into hiding on 6th July 1942, Moortje moved in with the family of one of Anne's friends. In a diary entry dated 12th July Anne describes how much she misses Moorjte and cries when she thinks of her. She also daydreams about their reunion. She might have had Moortje in mind when she addressed her diary as Dear Kitty, but Kitty could also have been a fictional character called Kitty Francken who featured in a series of popular Dutch books at the time. It probably didn't help Anne when the next day the van Pels family moved into the hiding place with their son Peter's cat Mouschi. According to Miep Gies, one of their helpers, the cat was an affectionate, friendly black tom cat. After the Nazis raided the hiding place, Mouschi remained in residence but missed Peter so much he was eventually adopted by the office cleaner. Two other cats who visited the hideaway were Tommy and Moffie, warehouse cats. In the original translation of Anne's diaries Moffie was called Boche as he picked fights with Tommy (a name used to describe British soldiers). Boche was a slang term used by the French to describe the Germans in World War I. Translators struggled to find an adequate translation for Moffie which is why most people believe the cat was called Boche. But the explanation for the cat's real name of Moffie lies with Miep Gies' description of him as a big, fat black and white tomcat whose face was bashed about due to his fights with other cats. A biscuit in the shape of a fat little pig was called a Moffen and this is what the Dutch called the Germans during the war. In the same way that the Germans were stealing food from the Dutch, so Moffie stole food from houses in the neighbourhood. The cat's appearance also helped to determine his name, being not dissimilar in shape or size to a pig, apart from the fur of course. He must have endeared himself somewhat to the household as Moffie is a far more affectionate derivative of Moffen.

BILL CLINTON American President
1946 - extant

Socks, the family pet cat of the Clintons became one of the most famous presidential cats of recent times.

A cartoon version of him guided children around the White House website. He was a black and white stray kitten who lived under the front porch of the house of Chelsea's piano teacher in Little Rock, Arkansas. Adopted by the Clintons, he moved into the White

House in 1993. During his time as the presidential cat he received large amounts of fan mail. Several books, one by Hillary Clinton, have been written about him. He was featured heavily in the media, turning up on songs, in sitcoms and cartoons. Socks also appeared alongside Bill Clinton in a set of stamps issued by the Central African Republic. The traditional enmity between cats and dogs eventually became his downfall when the Clintons' new chocolate Labrador puppy Buddy arrived. Socks and Buddy were enemies and when the Clintons left the White House in 2001 it was Socks' nemesis, Buddy, who was chosen by the Clintons to become the family's No.1 pet. Happily, Socks was given a home by Betty Currie, the President's secretary. Despite Socks' massive rejection by his adopted family and the loss of celebrity, he lived a long and pampered life, finally going to sleep for the last time in February 2009.

JOHN LENNON, *Musician*
1940-1980

John Lennon's love of cats began early, during his childhood in Liverpool. Whilst living with his Aunt Mimi and Uncle George he had three – Tich, Tim and Sam. He would cycle to the fishmongers to buy hake for them. Although not living with his mother, Julia, he would visit her often and she also had a cat, called Elvis.

Despite Elvis producing a litter of kittens, John's mother didn't change her name. After leaving home and getting married he insisted, according to his first wife Cynthia, on getting a cat. This was a tabby called Mimi, named after his beloved aunt. More followed, including Babaghi, until they had about 10 cats. Wherever he lived he would always have cats around him. When he left his second wife Yoko Ono for 18 months to live with May Pang in California, he had a black and a white pair of cats called Major and Minor. John and Yoko also cared for another pair of black white cats called Salt and Pepper. Sadly, John's favourite cat, a Russian blue called Alice jumped out of an open window of their Dakota apartment. John was distraught. His son Sean said that this was the only time he saw his father cry. Towards the end of his life John and Yoko owned a further 3 cats called Misha, Sasha and Charo. In total he owned and loved 17 cats. John loved to draw his cats and used many of them as illustrations in the book he wrote for Sean, *Real Love – the Drawings for Sean* (1999).

GEORGE HARRISON *Musician*
1943-2001

Like his fellow Beatle, George Harrison was a cat lover. He had Korky, a white Persian and Rupert and Joss Stick, both Siamese. At George's home, Friar Park in

Henley-on-Thames, his son Dani recalls how his father
would sit and meditate on a bench in the Japanese
garden. The neighbourhood cats would come into the
garden through a gap in the fence and sit and watch him
– quite possibly mesmerised by his calm and still
manner.

FREDDIE MERCURY, M*usician*
1946-1991
Anyone who saw Freddie Mercury perform
with Queen will understand why his flamboyant,
charismatic and outrageous personality captivated
millions of fans. In his private life, Freddie was, in some

ways, the opposite of his onstage alter-ego and was quite shy and reserved. Whilst he was surrounded by adoring fans onstage, away from the spotlight he was happiest when he was at home with his many cats. This feline love affair began when Freddie lived with Mary Austin, his lifelong friend and partner for 7 years. They owned a pair of cats called Tom and Jerry, but when they separated, Mary got the cats. In exchange, she gave Freddie a beautiful longhaired bluepoint he called Tiffany. At least two of his cats were adopted from The Blue Cross whilst others were given to him by friends and boyfriends. Oscar, a ginger and white tom, originally belonged to a boyfriend. On discovering his infidelity Freddie broke up with the lover but kept his cat. Freddie professed his love for his cats and everyone who loves cats on his solo album *Mr. Bad Guy* (1985) which was 'dedicated to my cat Jerry - also Tom, Oscar and Tiffany, and all the cat lovers across the universe – screw everybody else!' In 1987 Freddie adopted Delilah, a tri-coloured tabby who, it seems, proceeded to rule the roost at Garden Lodge, Mercury's London home. Whilst being a bully to the other cats she was always the first on Freddie's lap and loved to sleep on his bed. He wrote a song about her called *Delilah* which appeared on *Innuendo* (1991), the last album Freddie recorded with Queen. Goliath, a black cat, was also adopted at the same time as Delilah. He had a habit of sleeping in the marble sink in the bathroom and dribbling. Another tabby, Miko was named after a trip to Japan. Romeo, a white-faced tabby, was found by Freddie's boyfriend Jim Hutton. Romeo turned out to be not a lover but a fighter. Freddie's ambition to have a white cat was finally fulfilled when Lily joined his household to make his cat family complete. Whilst travelling the world Freddie would ring up to 'talk' to his cats. He spoilt them with individual stockings at Christmas filled with cat treats and toys. Most of the time they would eat fresh chicken and fish specially prepared for them. They had total freedom to roam the house and substantial gardens. These pampered and loved cats were extremely important to Freddie and after his death he ensured that they would not be disrupted or split up. He left most of his fortune to his beloved friend Mary Austin and she moved into Garden Lodge to care for them.

JEANETTE WINTERSON, *Author*
1959-extant

When Jeanette Winterson published her autobiography *Why Be Happy When You Could Be Normal* (2012) she revealed an extraordinary story about how one of her cats saved her life. In 2007 she was suffering from deep personal emotional anxiety and anguish and decided to commit suicide. The practicalities meant that as she was sitting in her car, slipping into unconsciousness, she felt her cat scratching her face. This intervention and the knowledge that the cat was locked in the car with her meant that she stumbled out of the car and found herself lying on her gravel drive. There are many cat owners who often say that having a cat saved their life, but not many for whom that is literally true.

Jeanette wrote movingly about putting her favourite cat Hopeful to sleep in May 2004. Equally distressing is her column about the death of Minnie, who was run down outside her house in October 2006. Silver brought new life into Jeanette's home when she had a litter of kittens in May 2005. Sadly, Silver died in August 2020 and Winterson tweeted 'That cat was my longest and most successful relationship. 16 years. It's not all about humans'.

TRACEY EMIN, *Artist*
1963-extant

In 2002 Tracey was given a kitten by a boyfriend and called it Docket. This kitten grew up to become her friend, companion, inspiration, and love of her life.

In March 2002 Docket went missing and like a lot of desperate owners of lost cats, she put up posters of her missing cat on streets and lamp posts near her home. Thinking the posters were original, valuable works of art by Tracey, some people tore them down in order to sell them. The story then featured on the front pages of *The Times* and *International Herald Tribune*. Fortunately, 6 days later there was a happy ending when Docket was found inside a derelict house. Docket became a feature of Tracey's art. In 2012 she made a bronze sculpture called *Docket in My Hand*. She travelled to Venice so she could immortalise him in glass, a piece that sold for £25,000. He was featured in paintings and ceramics and was a constant source of love and comfort. Unfortunately, in February of 2020, Docket died and, as all animal lovers know, the pain of losing your friend is immense. He was 19 and so lived a long and no doubt pampered life and will live on in the many art works he inspired.

About the Author

Christina Hamilton worked in television production at the BBC for 30 years. She travelled extensively as a Production Manager, on a wide range of classic documentaries for the Music and Arts Department. In 1991 she moved to the Natural History Unit in Bristol where she was a Production Executive on the BBC-2 series *The Natural World*. In 2003 she returned to her home city of Hull. She freelanced as a Producer/Director whilst studying part time at The University of Hull, graduating 6 years later with a First Class BA (Hons) in Arts and Humanities. She combines writing with her interest in history and art history and is looking forward to future writing projects. Her love for ice cream is second only to cats.

Acknowledgements

The first and most thanks are to Stephanie Zia at Blackbird Digital Books. This is the second book I have written about cats and their famous owners. When the feline muse was waning, Stephanie always gently encouraged me and has been endlessly patient. My thanks must also go to Natasha and Christian for allowing a picture of their gorgeous Chloe to be on the cover. Finally, thanks to my enthusiastic friends and family.

Picture Credits

Cover: Chloe by Christian Dalton-Locke, c. Christian Dalton-Locke

Dedication: *Rosie* colour photo, c. Christina Hamilton

Chapter 1

The Obsequies of an Egyptian Cat Painting by John Weguelin (1849 - 1927) Mackelvie Trust Collection, Auckland Art Gallery Toi o Tāmaki - no known copyright restrictions. http://www.aucklandartgallery.com/the-collection/browse-artwork/11228/the-obsequies-of-an-egyptian-cat

Unknown – The Japanese book (Tenno hyakunijuyondai) in Bessatsu-Taiyo, Heibonsha 1988 https://bit.ly/3k03LDn Public Domain

Chapter 2

Floor mosaic from House of the Faun, Pompeii.Cat with bird. Ducks and sea life. Museo Archeologico Nazionale Napoli Inv. 9993

Chapter 3

A pen and ink illustration of a cat in a tree, being harassed by a man and his dogs. From a late 15th Century CE manuscript made in Germany (probably Trier).
From Ms. Ludwig XV 1 (83.MR.171), fol. 48, in the collection of the Getty Museum.
Getty Museum Open Contents Program

Chapter 4

Portrait of a young lady holding a cat Francesco Bacchiacca (1494–1557) circa 1525. Private collection, public domain

Sir Isaac Newton B/W book illustration, taken from *The National and Domestic History of England (Vol 3)* (1878) Aubrey, William Hickman Smith. Public Domain.   http://www.fromoldbooks.org/Aubrey-HistoryOfEngland-Vol3/pages/vol3-401-Sir-Isaac-Newton/

Chapter 5

Statue of Dr Johnson's Cat, colour photo.
http://www.geograph.org.uk/photo/1713195
Dr Johnson's cat Hodge, Gough Square. copyright Kim Traynor and licensed for reuse under Creative Commons Licence.

The Young Marie-Antoinette 1769 Portrait by Joseph Ducreux pastel
Versaille. Image in public domain taken from Wikipedia

Robert Southey by Thomas Lawrence 1810
https://www.wikiart.org/en/thomas-lawrence/robert-southey-1810/
Public domain

Abraham Lincoln, three-quarter length portrait, by Anthony Berger 1864 Source
http://hdl.loc.gov/loc.pnp/ppmsc.00052 Public Domain

Charles Dickens in 1850 b/w photograph Author unknown Public Domain

Chapter 6

Alexandre Dumas 1855 photograph by Felix Nadar (a pseudonym of Gaspard-Félix Tournachon)

Victor Hugo circa 1875 photograph by Comte Stanisław Julian Ostroróg dit WALERY

Edgar Allen Poe June 1849 Daguerreotype 'Annie', given to Poe's friend Mrs. Annie L. Richmond. Photographer unknown

First Cat Show 1871 in London b/w photo, public domain

Florence Nightingale between 1900 and 1910, from a photo taken between 1860 and 1870
United States Washington Library of Congress's Prints and Photographs division Public Domain

Mr Clemmens and His Kitten (Mark Twain) b/w photo, 1907. Underwood & Underwood. Source The New York Times photo archive, Public Domain

Thomas Hardy & Cat from Dorset County Museum. Public Domain

Theodore Roosevelt, 1906 Official Nobel Peace Prize Photograph, Public Domain

Perce Blackburow with Mrs Chippy (Ship's cat on the 1914 Endurance expedition) b/w photo, Frank Hurley. Public Domain.

Statue of Mr Chippy. Colour photo Dec 2010. Author Nigel Cross. Gravestone of Harry McNeish in Karori Cemetery showing statue of Mrs Chippy. Public Domain

Marmalade cat, colour photograph by Charlene Simmons Flickr creative commons
Albert Einstein 1921 at a lecture in Vienna photograph by Ferdinand Schmutzer
Public domain

Chapter 7

Freddie Mercury performing in New Haven, CT,
16 November 1977. Creative Commons, CC BY-SA 3.

Tracey Emin at Lighthouse Gala Auction in aid of
Terrence Higgins Trust. Colour photograph by Piers
Allardyce. Creative Commons Attribution 2.0 Generic
license.

blackbird
blackbird-books.com

Printed in Great Britain
by Amazon

32919136R00066